LIFE IS A MARATHON... FINISH STRONG!

The Fitness Story of Donielle Spears

DONIELLE POLK SPEARS

LIFE IS A MARATHON...FINISH STRONG!

The Fitness Story of Donielle Spears

First Edition: April 2021

ISBN: 978-0-578-91270-7

"Therefore, since we are surrounded by such a great cloud of witnesses, let us throw off everything that hinders and the sin that so easily entangles. And let us run with perseverance the race marked out for us, fixing our eyes on Jesus, the pioneer and perfecter of faith." (Hebrews 12: 1-2)

DEDICATION

TO MY CHILDREN, DERRICK, JAMES, AND JAIME,
Life is full of obstacles. Keep your faith in God, never
give up, focus on the finish, and finish strong!

~Mom

CONTENTS

PREFACE

*Return to your home, and declare how much
God has done for you. And he went away pro-
claiming throughout the whole city how much
Jesus had done for him." (Luke 8: 39)*

SHARING YOUR STORY IS one of the most powerful means
that leaders and overcomers have to influence, teach, and
inspire. It forges connections among people and between
people and ideas. Jesus instructs us to share our story
and declare how much God has done for us. Every story
shared is a chance to make someone feel less alone. It
is with honor and excitement that I share my personal
salvation experience of overcoming obesity, finding success in running, and becoming an entrepreneur, while
battling marriage, self-destructing, seeking forgiveness,
and finding faith.

It's been a little over a year since our country endured the pandemic, COVID-19. Our country experienced life-changing challenges which helped Americans better understand and value life. We encountered hardships that affected our families, businesses, employees, our health, wealth, mental stability, and education to name a few.

Since the start of the pandemic, millions of people have experienced effective, virtual workouts in their homes and nutrition and fitness programs have been used more widely. Workout equipment and bicycles sold out nearly everywhere. Distributors like Amazon and Walmart were out of stock and backordered. Exercises like walking, running, and cycling have positive effects by preventing weight gain, reducing stress and anxiety, and improving sleep. Mental benefits include decreasing depression, sharpening memory, protecting the brain from aging, and boosting self-esteem.

Running is an amazing stress reliever. My path to physical fitness was challenging as I had to teach myself to run. Being a majorette in my high school and college band would make one think I was in good shape and running wouldn't be a challenge. I could march, I could twirl, I could dance, I was in good shape but I could not run. In fact, I hated it. However, positive thinking has physical effects on your body. It leaves you feeling optimistic, empowered to feel strong and confident, and increases your energy level. I was determined to learn and adapt to the consistent training stimulus.

I started my journey by enforcing this motto, "Your body will do whatever you set your mind to." If you want to become a runner, you will become a runner.

It started with defining and enforcing my "why." I set goals, surrounded myself with inspiration, celebrated small wins, and focused on health to help me remain consistent and committed. Being healthy became a part of my lifestyle.

I'm on a mission and in a position to help others. God has equipped me to succeed in His assignment. Every event recorded in this book is an experience of my own.

No longer trapped, having to calm my fears or nurture distractions, I have faced my past and defeated everything meant to tear me down. I have forgiven myself for the shortcomings and value the life lessons I've experienced. With every closed chapter, opened a new chapter, full of new beginnings, mercy and grace. By His power, I am still standing!

As you read, I encourage you to reflect on your own story. Think about times when you faced adversity and how you overcame. I have included focus questions to assist with documenting your testimony. I stand in full support of you and urge you to take control of *YOUR* life and *YOUR* health.

Remember to stand faithful in the word of God, and in all things, *FINISH STRONG!*

ACKNOWLEDGEMENTS

GOD, THE MOST HIGH, I thank you for giving me the vision, strength, courage, patience, and confidence to fulfill your assignment. Thank you for using me as a vessel to walk in my calling. May I continue to follow your lead, surrender unto you, and grow deeper in your word. —Amen

JAMES, my loving husband, thank you for your patience, understanding, and support throughout the many years. Thank you for never giving up on me and for loving me the way God requires us to love one another. You are the epitome of what I call a man, husband, father and friend. Your love for me is astonishing. Your patience is untouchable. I love you.

MYRA, my dear mother, you set the bar very high for me as a child. Thank you for showing me the path to success. Thank you for loving and supporting me on this journey called "Life." I love you.

ERVIN, my father, thank you for your commitment to understand me during my times of confusion. You have always encouraged me to be my very best and for that, I thank you. I love you.

EJ, my best friend and little brother, thank you for standing with me every step of the way. Thank you for helping me realize that nothing is impossible. You taught me to remind myself and live by your saying, "First is Last." I love you.

DERRICK, JAMES, AND JAIME, my three children, I am who I am because of you. I thank God for choosing me to be your mother. Thank you for loving me and for helping me understand my purpose and mission in life. I love you.

DR. RALPH M. MCCORMICK, my Pastor, thank you for your spiritual leadership and guidance. Thank you for being a great example of living in faith and blessing our church.

MCRAE CONSULTING, thank you for your support.

INTRODUCTION

WHEN WE THINK OF OR HEAR THE WORD "ADDICTION," most of the time, it's used in a negative context. Addiction is defined as "a compulsive need for and use of a habit-forming substance; an urge for something that is hard to control or stop." Many addictions are formed in an effort to hide behind a truth or a fact that we aren't ready to face. Are all addictions bad? The simple answer is no.

Imagine an addiction to running 26.2 miles at a time, two to three times a month. Family and friends wondering what has come over you and questioning what it is you're running from, while strangers watch in awe and brand a name for you globally. A wife and mother of three, if painting a picture to describe unbelievable, I'd be the picture.

It's May 28, 2016, my husband walks through the door as I walk out of the door. Passing by like roommates, the awkward silence filled the house like a glass of water. I arrived at the airport, boarded the plane and landed in Boston,

Massachusetts that evening. I picked up my rental car and headed to the state of Vermont to run my 10th marathon.

I approached the starting line the morning of Sunday, May 29, 2016. "On your mark, get set.... GO!" It was 92 degrees at 8am with an extremely high heat index. Runners passing out, water stations running out of water because of the overwhelming need for hydration, and continued sounds of sirens the entire race was beyond belief. Humidity makes running uncomfortable because the sweat cannot evaporate fast enough from our bodies. We tend to run slower because the body is working to prevent overheating. The humidity and lack of nutrients along the course caused me to fall slightly behind. At mile 13, I recall seeing the very person runners don't like to see during a road race, the "sweeper." You had to maintain a 13-minute pace and stay ahead of the sweeper in order to remain on the course. Once the sweeper passed, race equipment along the course was cleared, you were directed to clear the road, and could risk being disqualified. I had two options, clear the road or pick up the pace.

I made it!

At Mile 17, medic personnel flooded the race course to care for runners who seemed to be experiencing heat exhaustion. Race directors decided it was best to cancel the race. They sent buses along the course to pick up runners like me, runners who took precaution to lower their risk of overheating.

"But, I'm a runner. We don't quit."

In short, when things change, adjust. Adapt, move on, and keep going. As others had this same thought, a few of us decided to continue the race. Critics argued that we wouldn't receive an "official" race time and that we were automatically disqualified. Others, like myself, didn't worry about time or being disqualified. At this point in the race, giving up and quitting was not an option. To win, one must finish.

Mile 25, rain clouds filled the sky and raindrops began to fall. With a little over a mile left, we sped up as we had a clear sight of the finish line. A little over six hours, I FINISHED the 2016 Vermont City Marathon. Official or unofficial, I ran 26.2 miles… I ran a marathon!

How often are we faced with obstacles like these in our lives? Have you ever felt exhausted? Have you been in a situation that made you feel overheated? Have you experienced circumstances or people that made you feel less qualified? When we run into stumbling blocks, do we keep going or do we give up? Do we forfeit the battle or do we fight? Do we run away or do we face our challenges?

According to medical science, if you run a mile a day, you lower your risks of health concerns, improve your heart health, and obtain huge benefits.

Join me at the starting line for Lap 1 of my life.

LAP 1

The Race Begins

IT WAS AN EVENING IN JANUARY 2011. I undressed for the day and noticed a red mark across my abdomen. I continued to tell myself, "The dryer keeps shrinking my clothes." The mark darkened as each day passed, eventually, leaving a permanent bruise. Weeks of using lightning cream was only a temporary fix until I observed and identified the real issue and faced reality.

Obesity increases our risk of developing many potentially serious health conditions. Losing weight meant I had adapt to a new lifestyle to include:

- Eating a high protein breakfast
- Avoiding sugary drinks
- Drinking more water
- Making healthier food choices
- Eating soluble fiber

- Basing my diet on whole foods
- Eating slower
- Exercising

The list went on and on. Overwhelmed with the weight loss requirements, I consulted a doctor who specialized in weight loss. Appetite suppressants and supplements seemed ideal for me as I believed it would help curve my appetite and the result of "eating less" would result in weight loss. Exercising was difficult because "I didn't have time." If being a wife, with a husband who traveled for work, and a working mother of two toddlers wasn't enough on my plate, I was also attending Graduate School and finishing up my last semester. Cosmetically speaking, I didn't want to run the risk of sweating out my hair and adding extra visits to the hair salon either. My weight loss goal was 25 pounds and I wanted to achieve it without the hard work it required.

Running for My Life

"Good morning." I was greeted as I walked into the office for my first visit. I was excited as I filled out new patient forms, weighed in, and had a few tests administered. Shortly afterwards, the doctor walked into the room and there was an immediate feeling of uncertainty that I felt. He looked at me, looked at my chart, and said, "We have some concerns with your test results." With no idea of what those concerns were, I was puzzled.

I was referred to a Pulmonary Specialist. I wasn't fearful but I was confused. I tried searching the internet for reasons a patient may be referred to a Pulmonary Specialist. Here's what I found. "High blood pressure affecting the arteries in your lungs and in the right side of your heart is known as pulmonary hypertension." This was my diagnosis.

How did this happen? Why me? When did it happen? How long has this been an issue? What if I had not visited the doctor? What does this mean for me now? These were just a few questions running through my mind. So now, I had bigger issues than just weight loss. As the doctor continued to talk, I listened but heard nothing. My eyes locked into one spot on the wall for the remainder of my visit.

Studies show weight reduction to be quite beneficial in reducing pulmonary arterial pressures. The analytical side of me felt, "losing weight will beat this." My goal was to lose weight anyway, so now, I must choose the route I initially avoided, exercise and a healthy diet. This time, I was ready and motivated.

I learned of the 21/90 rule which is a method to building habits. Simply put, you commit to a goal for 21 days straight. After 21 days, the goal is established as a habit. Continue for another 90 days and you have effectively built a habit. I started on my journey. With numerous setbacks, but never giving up, by April, I mastered it!

I joined a local gym. On some days, I worked out twice a day. No longer worried about my hair, I felt accomplished. I participated in several fitness classes. My favorites were Zumba, Kickboxing, Step, and Cycling. Passing by the treadmill daily, there was no way I could run.

Graduation Day

Saturday, July 16, 2011, I walked across the stage and received my Masters of Arts in Education. I had also reached my 90-day mark and was 25 pounds lighter. By the end of 2011, I had lost over 60 pounds. A visit back to the Pulmonary Specialist resulted in no signs or symptoms of pulmonary hypertension. I defeated my diagnosis!

Change Lanes

Did you know that lack of proper nutrients hinders hair growth? I lost weight at a fairly rapid pace and while I understood the importance of confining calories for weight loss, perhaps excessive restriction resulted in hair loss. As a result, I lost a great amount of hair. It was about eight weeks since I had last relaxed my hair. Visually speaking, I had about an inch and a half of new (unrelaxed) hair. Then it happened…. The Big Chop! I looked in the mirror and thought, "Am I crazy?" I loved my hair. At a loss for words, I wasn't sure if I had lost my mind when I lost the weight. After a few weeks, I accepted my new look and thought, "Its hair, it'll grow back…I am not my hair."

As 2012 approached, I was in a state of extreme physical and mental fatigue. Headaches, tiredness, irritability, and sore muscles were signs of exhaustion. My commitment had become taxing on my body. Realizing that my adrenal gland, pumping out hormones as I exercised, can only produce so much cortisol at a time and the feeling of burnout influenced my decision to take a rest. My 8-month weight loss journey took a great amount of commitment and discipline and I was overexerted.

Did you know that approximately 80% of weight loss is nutrition, while 20% is exercise? While creating a calorific deficit, exercising will help speed up your metabolism and help you succeed in your weight loss journey. I followed the 80/20 rule and focused primarily on my diet. I increased my calorie consumption and provided my body the nutrition it needed and required. Ironically, I had more energy and felt better. More so, I witnessed my hair beginning to grow back.

After several months, I was ready to resume exercising. This time, I challenged myself to become a runner.

Focus Questions

1. What is your "Why?"

_____

_____

_____

_____

_____

_____

_____

_____

_____

_____

_____

_____

_____

2. What goal(s) do you want to achieve? How will you achieve your goal(s)?

_____

_____

_____

_____

_____

_____

_____

_____

_____

_____

_____

_____

_____

_____

_____

_____

3. What is your motivation? Someone? Something?

_____

_____

_____

_____

_____

_____

_____

_____

_____

_____

_____

_____

_____

_____

_____

_____

4. What exercises do you enjoy?

_____

_____

_____

_____

_____

_____

_____

_____

_____

_____

_____

_____

LAP 2

Pick Up the Speed

A NEW YEAR...TIME TO RESET. Resolutions help you reflect on the past, present, and future. They help you figure out what has worked, will work, or needs to be changed. Resolutions help give your goals a boost.

My resolution was to become a runner. Workouts offering a variety of intense exercises with brief recovery in between may encourage weight loss. Interval running helps improve your endurance by repeating short, intense runs with short breaks in between. They also help build speed and reduce fatigue. I began running intervals on the greenway with one of my best friends. There were times I felt discouraged and wanted to forfeit my resolution. My best friend had been running for a few months and she constantly encouraged me to keep going. We were on the weight loss journey together and had one common goal, to maintain our healthy lifestyle.

It was a beautiful spring day. We started off running. Normally, by mile one, we would take a break, but not this day. We ran the paved trails, under the bridges, and through the gravel. As we turned around to head back, I realized I had run the entire time. We approached our cars as my Nike running app stated my time, distance, and average pace. It was on this day that I realized, "**I am runner.**"

My best friend also encouraged me to join a local running group. Being that one of my initiatives was to surround myself with others like myself, I was excited. I met a lot of inspiring and motivating ladies. There were runners of all running levels. Some had been running for years, others were just like me, beginners. I met with this group consistently on Tuesday and Thursday evenings. Three miles turned into four, four miles turned into five, and five miles turned into six. I now had stamina and endurance to run six miles nonstop.

On September 8, 2013, my best friend and I ran our first official race, a 10K (6.2 miles), in Charlotte, North Carolina. Continuing to train myself and increase my distance, I finished the "Thunder Road Half Marathon" (13.1 miles) in November 2013.

Keep It Going

January 2014, I began running with another group of ladies within the same organization. We met every Monday,

Wednesday, and Friday at 5am. I wasn't sure I could handle the earlier morning runs but I was in love with the benefits:

- Beating the heat
- Fewer distractions
- More overall energy
- Better focus and mood
- Having appetite control

I was soon asked to assist the leader of the group by being a co-leader. This was BIG! Perhaps, my commitment and enthusiasm was admired and the leadership skill in me was evident. Ever had that feeling that your name was being mentioned in rooms you had no idea existed? That was the feeling I had and it felt good!

I was committed and I loved my position as a Run Coordinator. Volunteering gives people a sense of purpose. The feeling of giving back and contributing my time was unparalleled. This group was one of the largest, with an average of 40-50 ladies at each meetup. I was helping others achieve their goals through my leadership and dedication while becoming a better leader and runner. After leading the group alone for a couple months, I selected a co-lead to assist me.

Doing God's work is pleasing in His eyes. Those who do His work are heard, blessed, and rewarded. I began assisting my church's fitness ministry by leading a walk on Saturday mornings. To promote health and wellness within our church, I organized a race for my church's 100th anniversary. On June 7, 2014, over 100 members participated in the "100th Anniversary 5K!"

Ready for another road race, I entered the lottery to run the infamous "Peachtree Road Race" on July 4, 2014. I was selected and along with 60,000 other runners, I ran the streets of Atlanta, Georgia. Growing a deeper love for running, leading, and helping others, I registered for and completed an official training class to receive my certification in run coaching. In July 2014, I became a certified run coach through Road Runners Club of America (RRCA). This opportunity helped me empower people to run, but specifically, promote and train in distance running.

To prevent boredom and further challenge myself, I began swimming and cycling. As a result, I completed a Duathlon and Triathlon in the fall of 2014.

With so many accomplishments, even I was wondering what was next on the agenda. "Sacrifice is a part of every journey to become great." I decided to train for a Full Marathon. Coincidentally, my co-lead's goal was to run a marathon that year as well. I composed a 20-week training and she was my first (official) long distance trainee.

Run the first third with your head (Be Smart)
Run the second third with your legs (Be Strong)
Run the last third with your heart (Be Inspired)

November 15, 2014, approximately 5 hours and 14 minutes after we begin our race, I heard "Donielle Spears" as I crossed the finish line. The woman who hated running had become a Run Coordinator of a running group, a Certified Run Coach, trained another runner (and herself) for a full marathon, and became a part of the 1% of the world's population who has run and completed a FULL marathon!

In December, I proceeded to run two half marathons in two days in two different states (Huntersville, North Carolina and Atlanta, Georgia). I was now qualified as a "Half Fanatic."

The Insanity

"Half Fanatics" and "Marathon Maniacs" are "clubs for runners who are crazy about running and ready to take it to the next level." To become members of these groups, you had to qualify for the "insanity." For example, two full marathons had to be completed in 16 days to become a "Marathon Maniac." Having a running buddy to partake in all of this insanity made it even more fun.

After finishing the "Hall of Fame Marathon" in Canton, Ohio on April 26, 2015 and the "Good Life Fitness Marathon" in Toronto, Canada on May 2, 2015, I became a "Marathon Maniac." I was also an International Marathoner (finishing a marathon outside of the United States of America).

I joined several global running groups across social media. There, I posted my training runs and race pictures as well as met and networked with runners from all over the world. After a run or race, I would pose a flexed muscle to symbolize *strength* and *confidence*.

Short for Donielle and as symbol of power and control, I adopted the title, "The Don." I was a petite, young lady with such a powerful drive. Soon after, the name grew notoriety and was used by many.

Don't Stop Now

Did you know that travel improves social and communication skills, ensures peace of mind, helps you creatively think, broadens your horizons, boosts your confidence, and enhances your tolerable uncertainty? These were all the benefits I experienced while traveling to run road races outside of North Carolina. My co-lead became my running buddy and my friend. We entered the lottery for one of The Abbott World Major Marathons, "Bank of America Chicago Marathon." We got in! While training for Chicago, we ran several half marathons in other states including Atlanta, Georgia, Johnston, Tennessee, Virginia Beach, Virginia, Detroit, Michigan, and Brooklyn, New York.

The experience was breathtaking. I was executing my goals with confidence and my discipline continued to compound. I was becoming physically and mentally stronger as a runner. The accolades and attention was the first step in my learning process. "Hit The Don" became my signature pose and during races, I would hear my name being called while other runners were "Hitting The Don."

After running in seven states, one other country, and over 16 road races from November 2014 to October 2015, running had become costly. Factoring in unexpected expenses was another challenge. After missing our flights back home after the Chicago marathon, we were faced with additional lodging fees and flight tickets.

Stumbling Block (Finances)

A number of studies have demonstrated a link between financial worries and mental illnesses such as depression and anxiety. Financial burdens adversely impact your mental health. "The stress of debt or other financial issues can leave you depressed or anxious." Ever paid for a road race? Ever priced a road race? Imagine having to include lodging, travel, and food along with your race entry fees. Some races required leaving on Friday and returning on Monday, thus requiring days off from work and additional time away from family.

My budget didn't factor in all of these racing fees. In an effort to save on costs but still travel and run, I would plan day trips. While this saved on costs, close your eyes and image riding in the backseat of a car from Charlotte, North

Carolina to Huntington, West Virginia. You awake, grab a quick snack, and head to the starting line to run your fifth marathon. After the race, you head back home. Lack of sleep, body aches, and slower reaction time were all problems I began to encounter. Sure, it would've been easy to just say to myself, "stop running road races and stop traveling." But the art of running and running races helped manage stress, put me in a calmer state of mind, increased my productivity, decreased depression, and was a coping mechanism to all of life's issues.

I added another road race to my running journey as I finished a half marathon in Trenton, New Jersey (November 2015). Soon after, I ran my sixth marathon, "Route 66." A layover in Detroit, Michigan that would've landed us in Tulsa, Oklahoma the night prior to the race resulted in a canceled flight due to extreme weather conditions. Persistent to not give up, I was able to convince the agent at Gate D4 that we needed to get on the flight departing for Dallas, Texas. Upon boarding, I quickly reserved a rental car. We arrived in Dallas around midnight, secured our rental, and headed for Oklahoma. Down the dark roads with nothing in sight but our headlights…. BOOM! We hit a deer.

We had come too far. There was no turning back. We arrived in Tulsa around 730am, grabbed our race packets, and arrived at the starting line two minutes before the shotgun sounded. The plan was to fly back home immediately after the race (saving money on lodging expenses and reducing time away from family). However, running on primarily fumes due to the lack of sleep and feelings of exhaust made this impossible. Guess what? Another unexpected expense…An additional flight ticket.

Within two weeks, I had encountered two additional plane tickets, an additional night of lodging, race fees, and an increase in my insurance premium.

The Last Stretch

Taking time to figure out a budget to help fund my travel and races, I tried using the 50/30/20 rule. I used 50% on after-tax needs, 30% on wants and 20% on savings or paying a debt. Working part-time made it difficult to execute this budget efficiently, therefore, I was forced to use money I had set aside in my savings account. My thoughts were, "we save money to be able to use it for things we love or desire." With that in mind, on December 19, 2015, I became an Ultra Marathoner as I finished the "Houston Running Festival 50K" (31 miles) in Houston, Texas.

Continuing to lead the run group, traveling state to state, running race after race, I challenged myself to run a road race in all 50 states.

Here I come 2016!

Focus Questions

1. What is your level of commitment to exercise? Commitment to self-care?

_____

_____

_____

_____

_____

_____

_____

_____

_____

_____

_____

_____

_____

_____

_____

2. What are some of your major accomplishments?

_____

_____

_____

_____

_____

_____

_____

_____

_____

_____

_____

_____

_____

_____

_____

_____

_____

_____

3. Have you encountered stumbling blocks? How did you overcome them?

_____

_____

_____

_____

_____

_____

_____

_____

_____

_____

_____

_____

_____

_____

_____

LAP 3

Half Way There

JACKSON, MISSISSIPPI, MIAMI, FLORIDA, New Orleans, Louisiana, Little Rock, Arkansas, Washington, D.C., Annapolis, Maryland, and Salt Lake City, Utah, I was getting closer and closer to my goal of running the 50 states.

Some of my 2016 milestones include:

- A 200-mile relay race running from Santee, South Carolina to Charleston, South Carolina (March 2016);
- A 200-mile relay race running from Cumberland, Maryland to Washington, D.C. (September 2016);
- A 200-mile relay running from Raleigh, North Carolina to Atlantic Beach, North Carolina (October 2016);
- A total of 19 marathons
- Completing 12 of 50 states and D.C.

The support of the running community encouraged me to amplify my creative thinking on how to best merge my love for fashion and fitness into my lifestyle of running:

"The Don"
"Hit The Don"
"Fashion and Fitness"

And then came an idea…

RUNWITHMETOFASHION

Creating a career that aligns with my values, having a flexible schedule, meeting like-minded people, choosing who to work with, creating greater self-confidence, and having constant growth and development were reasons for me to launch my own business. This would allow me the opportunity to make money by doing what I love, have another stream of income, be my own boss, continue making an impact on people's life, and continue being a leader. I was a certified run coach, a world renowned runner, a marathoner, known for my fitness, and I had a supportive environment. The only thing missing was my initiative to brand myself and my business.

After finishing the Colorado Marathon in May 2016, in the snow, I decided to pause from racing for the remainder of the month to focus on my business strategy and plan.

I took a leap of faith and I did it!

On June 29, 2016, #HitTheDon "Strong, Confident... Fashionably Fierce!" —The Don (my logo) was filed with the United States Patent and Trademark Office.

On July 12, 2016 at 12:01pm, *RUNWITHMETOFASHION* was birthed and registered in the county of Mecklenburg, North Carolina.

"I Dreamed It…. Then, Real-Lifed It!"

RUNWITHMETOFASHION was publicly launched on July 29, 2016 at 8:14am offering a variety of services to include Run Coaching, Motivational Speaking, Personal Styling, and my #HitTheDon fitness apparel line.

On this journey of entrepreneurship, I learned so much about operating my own business. Just like a marathon, it was hard work, took persistence, dedication, patience, and confidence. On July 31, 2016, I ran the "San Francisco Marathon," wearing and showcasing my apparel with honor and in admiration of my accomplishments.

With such an outstanding fitness and weight loss journey as well as becoming a business owner, my story reached the masses.

- I was featured by Under Armor as one of their chosen "Athlete Spotlights"
- I was a guest speaker on WBND Radio

- I attended and served as an orator for "Go Red Awareness"
- I hosted a workshop (Entrepreneurship 101) for young teens

Fall 2016, I created my personal training group (#TeamDon), where I volunteered hours of training to ladies (and gentlemen). I showcased my business in September 2016 by organizing a "sold out" fashion show presented by *RUNWITHMETOFASHION*.

Painful Success

Pain makes you grow. Pain has its own noble joy. In my growing and in my joy lived pain.

What was this pain?

No matter how liberated or self-sufficient we are, moods and behaviors demonstrated by our loved ones affect our health. We are made to need an emotional connection. When we are married, we need to feel the love from our partner and in turn, reciprocate that same love. Having nothing to say to each other, being with one another but not being there for one another, becoming preoccupied with other people's needs and emotions, growing distant, encountering relationship destroyers, feeling unheard, going to friends instead of your spouse, lacking quality time, and remembering date nights as a "thing of the past," were all signs I felt through my pain.

Alongside the pain was the struggle of balancing a new business, an unhealthy marriage, financial burdens, and running.

In the midst of success, there may be pain.
In the midst of growing, there will be setbacks.
In the midst of living your dream, you may become selfish.

In the midst of lifestyle changes, things of importance may become neglected.

In the midst of refining, we find new discoveries.

When there seems to be clear vision, the very thing that may be missing is clarity.

For me, I was happy. I was glowing. But I was unhappy, sinking,
and in a dark place.

I loved helping others. But I couldn't help myself or my marriage.

I became selfish and poured into those who seemed to pour into me. I was finding success in running while battling the loss of my marriage.

Focus Questions

1. Have you ever felt overwhelmed? How did you overcome it?

_____

_____

_____

_____

_____

_____

_____

_____

_____

_____

_____

_____

_____

_____

2. Has there been a time when you felt like your success was the outcomes of other's expectations and not your own?

_____

_____

_____

_____

_____

_____

_____

_____

_____

_____

_____

_____

_____

_____

_____

3. Do you have a fitness budget?

_____

_____

_____

_____

_____

_____

_____

_____

_____

_____

_____

_____

_____

_____

_____

_____

4. What is your dream? What will it take to achieve your dream?

_____

_____

_____

_____

_____

_____

_____

_____

_____

_____

_____

_____

_____

_____

_____

_____

LAP 4

Endangered of a "DNF" (Do not finish)

"I therefore, a prisoner for the Lord, urge you to walk in a manner worthy of the calling to which you have been called." (Ephesians 4:1)

DO YOU KNOW WHAT GOD REQUIRES OF YOU? Do you know your calling? Are you walking in your calling? Often times, we take God's plan and alter it to best suit our personal needs. The blessing was that I found and walked in my calling. However, failing to follow God's path left me lost, hopeless, and disappointed.

Running Away

On our wedding day, my pastor said, "The same love it took to get you to the altar is not the same love that will keep you together."

We weren't the same individuals that we were over 20 years ago. Traveling for work left me feeling like a single mother, the lack of communication left me doubtful, the lack of support left me frustrated, and the lack of attention left me irritable. Running helped me cope with all of the emotions and feelings I had bottled up for so long. I was able to fight this battle through running. I had no fight in me.... Better yet, I chose not to fight and I wasn't alone. The "teenage love" wasn't enough to hold the pieces of us together. Everything fell apart and we went our separate ways.

During the time of separation, I often asked myself if it was the weight loss, the running, the travel, the attention... "Was it just me?" For me, it was the lack of support and attention. For him, it was the lack of balance and prioritization. These imbalances and imperfections left us both vulnerable and although we wanted to act on our insecurities and vulnerabilities, that was rather selfish. We didn't do the same things together and everything about our marriage became predictable. We did nothing to ignite passion into our marriage. We were both a running a race; A race of our own.

I found myself trying to replace missing parts of my life but yet I was sinking deeper and deeper. I remained confident, smiling on the outside, but was lost on the inside. Happiness is vital to our own goals in life and can help us achieve personal ambitions. Being happy allows us the potential to change the lives of others but more so, change our own lives. Did I know what it took to make "Donielle" happy? It was time to refine me.

Finding Donielle

Finding yourself isn't a one-time thing and we require daily check-ins with self. I began my journey of self-happiness. Distractions are inevitable but I was focusing on the keys to happiness, including:

- Being around others who made me smile
- Holding to my values
- Accepting the good and imagining the best
- Doing things I loved
- Finding purpose
- Listening to my heart
- Pushing myself

I made progress but still questioned God about my life feeling like complete punishment. I realized that I was missing one-on-one time with God. I wasn't praying as I should and I wasn't asking God for help. I wasn't specific to what I needed. Even though God knew what I wanted and needed, he wanted me to ask him for it. I began to pray more and God answered those vague prayers but being specific created a deeper bond between God and I.

The first step to self-reconstruction is admitting and accepting your flaws. The next step is to forgive yourself for falling short. I began to see my perceived flaws in a new light, realizing that acceptance was my only option for truly loving myself. Acceptance allowed me to measure things in the right perspective. Accepting my flaws disqualified others' opinions of me. During this process, I learned that nothing was completely good but nothing was completely bad. Practicing gratitude, recognizing that I am not my thoughts, helped me on this path of reconstruction. I framed my reality more soundly rather than on a false motion of self.

In order to heal, I had to forgive. Feelings of understanding, empathy, and compassion for self were results of forgiveness. I didn't have to forget to forgive, I forgave for peace to be able to continue on with life. It was for my own growth and led me to a path of letting go of hurt, pain, resentment, and anger. Forgiveness freed me to live in the present.

In my healing process, I remembered how important it was to "do what you love." I started 2017 running the "Charleston Marathon" (South Carolina) on January 14, 2017. February 11, 2017, I finished the "Hilton Head Marathon" (South Carolina), traveled to Birmingham, Alabama and ran the "Mercedes Benz" marathon on February 12, 2017. I loved racing but this process of healing forced me to take a step back. Rather than running 50 states, I decided to complete *35 marathons by my 35th birthday* and then, retire from distance running.

- Marathon 31 (March 5, 2017) —"Little Rock Marathon" (Little Rock, Arkansas)
- Marathon 32 (March 19, 2017) —"Publix Marathon" (Atlanta, Georgia).

After my 32nd marathon, I decided I was done. No more marathons.

Thirty-Three; Thirty-Four

"Though I am surrounded by troubles, you will bring me safely through them." (Psalm 138:7)

While in this process of refining "me," the enemy was attacking my character and integrity at full speed. Still on an emotional roller coaster, I learned that I couldn't make everything happen in my own strength. It was time to take a seat and allow God to stand on my behalf and go to work. Through prayer and faith, I knew God would direct my path and not allow me to give up.

July 2017, God began speaking to me. Through feelings of peace and through the influence of the Holy Spirit, I felt God's presence in my heart. August 2017 (14 months after being separated), I was at a place of rest and ready to fight "the good fight."

Studies show that approximately 13% of couples are able to reconcile post-separation. Thankful to be in that number, the road to reconciliation allowed us to create a plan of action, reflecting on outcomes. We identified what went wrong, evaluated our relationship, discussed needs and expectations, created healthy boundaries, identified root issues, and controlled anger and blaming. We began dating, looking to the future, slowly picked up the pieces worth keeping, and moved forward. Our separation was a great way to process our individual issues.

My friend asked me to run one last marathon with her. With the support of my husband, I ran my 33rd marathon on October 15, 2017, the "Nationwide Children's Hospital Columbus Marathon" (Columbus, Ohio), adding state number 26 to my portfolio.

The year ended on November 5, 2017 as I crossed the finish line of another World Major, the "New York City Marathon" (Marathon 34), as my husband stood close to finish line waiting for "us." I received my medal and surrendered to the Almighty for covering me and my six week old embryo. I was pregnant!

Lap 4 complete.

Focus Questions

1. Have you found yourself running from a problem? How did you manage or how are you managing it?

_____

_____

_____

_____

_____

_____

_____

_____

_____

_____

_____

_____

_____

_____

_____

_____

_____

2. What is effective communication? What have you done to ensure the lines of communication remain open between you and a significant other?

_____

_____

_____

_____

_____

_____

_____

_____

_____

_____

_____

_____

_____

_____

_____

3. Have you ever felt like giving up? If yes, write it down and talk about how you pulled through.

FINISH STRONG

"But those who trust in the Lord will find new strength. They will soar high on wings like eagles. They will run and not grow weary. They will walk and not faint." (Isaiah 40:31)

BEING A MOTHER OF TWO BOYS, I was excited to hear I was having my girl! I was specific in my prayer to God (for a healthy baby girl). I continued to manage my business, *RUNWITHMETOFASHION,* and after publicly announcing my reconciliation, I released another motivation tee which broke record sales:

#God

#Family

…Everything else

It's important that we recognize and accept that the Lord will cause "the iniquity of us all to fall on Him" (Isaiah 53:

4-6). Without the presence of God, we will continue to fight our demons and remain "lost in the power of darkness of sin until God transforms us."

There is no success or transformation without work, pain, suffering, and a sense of loss.

During my time of refining, I identified the necessary tools to help me navigate through life. I refer to these tools as the "*7 Pillars of Survival.*"

- Faith
- Family
- Finance
- Fitness
- Forgiveness
- Mental Health
- Self-Care

It wasn't until I allowed God into my life again that I was able to begin my journey of peace, face my past and accept my present. Accepting my present is allowing me to better my future.

As I stated in the introduction, I ran into stumbling blocks during the Vermont City Marathon. However, I didn't allow anything to deter me from finishing the race. The warmer temperature, the heat index, the lack of hydration, the sounds of sirens, the sweeper, pick up buses along the route, the announcement of a canceled race, and even the cloudy skies were reasons for me to give up. And as in life, hurt, pain, resentment, disappointment, self-destruction, vulnerabilities, and uncertainties could've held me captive but I fought on, took a seat, and allowed God to go to work on my behalf.

2018, before my 36th birthday, I realized that I had met my goal of running 35 marathons. My longest, toughest, most valued, and my favorite marathon... God saved the BEST for last. The "Marathon of Life" saved my marriage and my family. My 35th marathon was complete! I finished a better woman of God, wife to my husband, and mother to my sons and unborn daughter.

The woman who started the race was not the same woman who finished the race!

YOUR LIFE IS YOUR MARATHON... FINISH STRONG!

To God be the glory!

	Monday	Tuesday	Wednesday	Thursday	Friday	Saturday	Sunday
Week 1	Run 1 minute Walk 1 minute Repeat x 9	Rest Day	Run 2 minutes Walk 1 minute Repeat x 7	Rest Day	Cross Training Day	Run 2 minutes Walk 1 minute Repeat x 10	Rest Day
Week 2	Run 3 minutes Walk 1 minute Repeat x 8	Rest Day	Run 3 minutes Walk 45 seconds Repeat x 10	Rest Day	Cross Training Day	Run 4 minutes Walk 1 minute Repeat x 7	Rest Day
Week 3	Run 5 minutes Walk 45 seconds Repeat x 6	Rest Day	Run 6 minutes Walk 1 minute Repeat x 7	Rest Day	Cross Training Day	Run 7 minutes Walk 45 seconds Repeat x 5	Rest Day
Week 4	Run 8 minutes Walk 1 minute Repeat x 7	Rest Day	Run 10 minutes Walk 30 seconds Repeat x 5	Rest Day	Cross Training Day	Run 10 minutes Walk 30 seconds Repeat x 6	Rest Day
Week 5	Run 9 minutes Walk 30 seconds Repeat x 6	Rest Day	Run 11 minutes Walk 30 seconds Repeat x 5	Rest Day	Cross Training Day	Run 12 minutes Walk 30 seconds Repeat x 4	Rest Day
Week 6	Run 15 minutes Walk 30 seconds Repeat x 3	Rest Day	Run 11 minutes Walk 30 seconds Repeat x 4	Rest Day	Cross Training Day	5K Race!	Celebrate!

VIRTUAL 5K TRAINING

Created by Coach D (Donielle Polk Spears)

Successful runners cross-train to help combat boredom and rest the runner's foot. Cross-training helps lead to a better, injury-free performance. Rest is equally important.

This training plan recommends one day of cross training and two days of rest.

Note: This is a general guide and should be used to best suit each individual.

Seven cross-training exercises for runners: Cycling, Swimming, Elliptical, Walking, Strength Training

HEALTH AND WELLNESS JOURNAL

_____

_____

_____

_____

_____

_____

_____

_____

_____

_____

_____

_____

_____

_____

_____

_____

FINISH STRONG!

_____

_____

_____

_____

_____

_____

_____

_____

_____

_____

_____

_____

_____

_____

_____

_____

_____

_____

FINISH STRONG!

_____

_____

_____

_____

_____

_____

_____

_____

_____

_____

_____

_____

_____

_____

_____

_____

_____

_____

_____

_____

_____

_____

_____

_____

_____

_____

_____

_____

_____

_____

_____

_____

_____

_____

_____

_____

FINISH STRONG!

_____

_____

_____

_____

_____

_____

_____

_____

_____

_____

_____

_____

_____

_____

_____

_____

_____

_____

_____

_____

_____

_____

_____

_____

_____

_____

_____

_____

_____

_____

_____

_____

_____

_____

_____

_____

_____

_____

FINISH STRONG!

FINISH STRONG!

_____

_____

_____

_____

_____

_____

_____

_____

_____

_____

_____

_____

_____

_____

_____

_____

_____

_____

Made in the USA
Columbia, SC
23 May 2021